How to Draw
Minnesota's
Sights and Symbols

Jaycee Kuedee

The Rosen Publishing Group's
PowerKids Press™
New York

For Grant Quasha

Published in 2002 by The Rosen Publishing Group, Inc.
29 East 21st Street, New York, NY 10010

First Edition

Book Design: Kim Sonsky
Layout Design: Dean Galiano
Project Editor: Jannell Khu

Illustration Credits: Jamie Grecco
Photo Credits: p. © 7 Bill Ross/CORBIS; p. 8 (photo) © photo by Lee Brothers, Minnesota Historical Society, (sketch) © The Minneapolis Institute of Arts; p. 9 © The Minneapolis Institute of Arts; pp. 12, 14 © One Mile Up, Incorporated; p. 16 © Hal Horwitz/CORBIS; p. 18 © Robert Estall/CORBIS; pp. 20, 24 © Gunter Marx/CORBIS; p. 22 © Richard Hamilton Smith/CORBIS; p. 26 giant beaver illustrated by Charles Douglas reproduced with permission of the Canadian Museum of Nature, Ottawa, Canada; p. 28 © Joseph Sohm; ChromoSohm Inc./CORBIS.

Kuedee, Jaycee
How to draw Minnesota's sights and symbols / Jaycee Kuedee.
p. cm. — (A kid's guide to drawing America)
Includes index.
Summary: This book explains how to draw some of Minnesota's sights and symbols, including the state seal, the official flower, and the state capitol building located in St. Paul.
  ISBN 0-8239-6079-X
1. Emblems, State—Minnesota—Juvenile literature 2. Minnesota—In art—Juvenile literature   3. Drawing—Technique—Juvenile literature [1. Emblems, State—Minnesota   2. Minnesota 3. Drawing—Technique]
I. Title   II. Series
  2001
  743'.8'99776—dc21

Manufactured in the United States of America

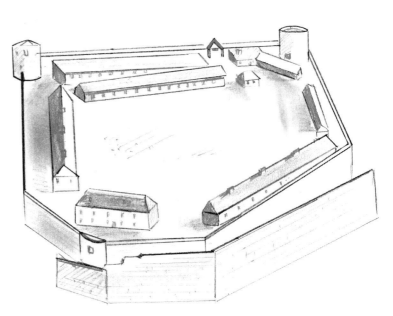

CONTENTS

Let's Draw Minnesota

The state of Minnesota was named for the Minnesota River, which is located in the southern area of the state. The name "Minnesota" comes from the Native American word *mnishota*, which means "cloudy" or "milky water." Native Americans lived on the state's land long before French fur trader and explorer Pierre Radisson reached the area in 1654. Radisson and his brother-in-law, Médard Chouart des Groseilliers, were the first-known Europeans to have set foot in the area now known as Minnesota. By 1695, the French built forts all around the state that later would be called Minnesota. These forts included Isle Pelee, built in 1695, Fort L'Huillier, built in 1700, and Fort Beauharnois, built in 1727. In 1763, the British took control of the eastern part of Minnesota. After the American Revolution, the United States gained control of this area. In 1803, the western part of Minnesota was bought from France as part of the Louisiana Purchase.

In 1849, Minnesota became an American territory and in 1858, Minnesota became a state. By the late

1800s and early 1900s, many Europeans from Germany, Sweden, and Norway settled in Minnesota.

You will learn more about Minnesota and its many sights and symbols by reading this book. To draw Minnesota's sights and symbols, follow these simple tips. All of the drawings begin with a basic shape. From there you will add other shapes. Directions help explain how to do all the steps. Each new step of the drawing is shown in red to help guide you. The supplies you will need to draw Minnesota's sights and symbols are:

- A sketch pad
- An eraser
- A number 2 pencil
- A pencil sharpener

These are some of the shapes and drawing terms you need to know to draw Minnesota's sights and symbols:

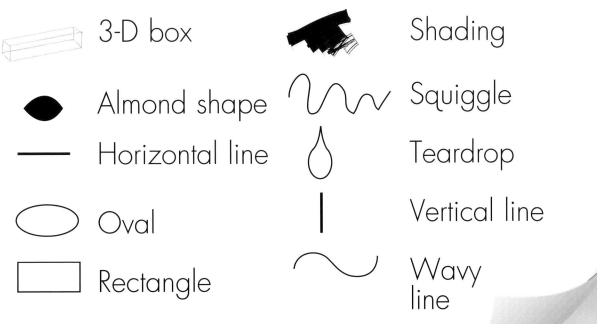

3-D box

Shading

Almond shape

Squiggle

Horizontal line

Teardrop

Oval

Vertical line

Rectangle

Wavy line

Star of the North

Minnesota's nickname comes from the state motto, *l'etoile du nord*, which means the "star of the north" in French. This nickname comes from an area in Minnesota known as the Northwest Angle, the northernmost point of the 48 contiguous states. Minnesota has other nicknames, such as the Land of 10,000 Lakes, even though it has almost 12,000 lakes. It is called the Gopher State because Minnesota is home to many gophers. Another nickname is the Bread and Butter State, because the state produces a lot of wheat and dairy products. Minnesota is known for its twin cities, Minneapolis and St. Paul. In fact the state's American League baseball team, the Minnesota Twins, is named for the twin cities. Just outside of the Twin Cities is Bloomington, home of the Mall of America. The mall has more than 500 stores, an indoor amusement park, the state's largest aquarium, a motor speedway, and 14 movie theaters! More than 40 million people visit the mall every year.

The Mississippi River is the largest river in North America. The Mississippi River runs through downtown Minneapolis.

Artist in Minnesota

Robert Koehler

Robert Koehler was born in Germany in 1850. He was three years old when his family moved to Wisconsin. Koehler studied art in New York City and continued his studies in Germany, where he worked and lived for 13 years. In 1893, the Minneapolis School of Fine Arts invited Koehler to join its staff and in 1894, he became the school's second art director. In the late nineteenth century, Koehler was one of a group of painters who spread a new art trend in America that gave a "real-life" view of the Industrial Revolution. The Industrial Revolution began in England in the 18th century. It changed the

Koehler sketched *Prosit!* in 1886. Prosit means to wish good health, especially before drinking.

way people lived and worked due to the invention and use of machines and the growth of factories. An example of such change is that many areas in America shifted from rural communities to urban cities. This was the kind of change Koehler captured in his paintings. You can see this in the painting below, which he painted around 1910. All the buildings in the painting were built around 1880, when the city thrived from commercial development, such as lumbering, flour milling, and trade. The big building behind the tree is the Minneapolis Public Library, which housed the Minneapolis School of Fine Arts. Robert Koehler died in 1917 at the age of 67.

Rainy Evening on Hennepin Avenue was done in oil on canvas and measures 24" x 25 ¾" (61 cm x 65 cm). The woman and child in the foreground are Koehler's wife and son, with the family dog!

Map of Minnesota

Map of the Continental United States

Minnesota covers 86,943 square miles (225,181 sq km) of land. It is located in the northern part of the Midwest and borders North Dakota, South Dakota, Iowa, Wisconsin, and the country of Canada. The major rivers in the state are the Mississippi River, the Minnesota River, the Red River, and the St. Croix River. The state has 6,564 rivers and streams and 11,842 lakes. That's a lot of water! Eastern Minnesota borders one of the Great Lakes, Lake Superior. Eagle Mountain, in the northeast area of the state, is the highest point and measures 2,301 feet (701 m) above sea level. It is located in Superior National Forest, one of two national forests in the state. The other is the Chippewa National Forest.

1

Draw a rectangle.

2

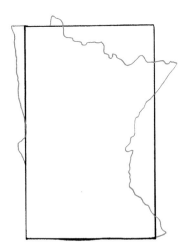

Use the rectangle as a guide and draw the shape of Minnesota.

3

Erase extra lines. Draw a circle for Minneapolis. To mark Minneopa State Park, draw a triangle.

4

Let's continue to draw some of Minnesota's key places. Now draw two connected, wavy ovals for the upper and lower Red Lakes. For the F. Scott Fitzgerald House, draw a square.

5

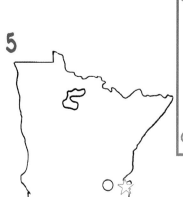

☆	St. Paul
○	Minneapolis
△	Minneopa State Park
▢	F. Scott Fitzgerald House
⬡	Upper and lower Red Lakes

To finish your map, draw a star to mark Minnesota's capital, St. Paul. You can also draw the map key. Use the map key to make sure you drew all the key points in the right locations. Good job!

The State Seal

   Minnesota's state seal was adopted in 1861, three years after the state joined the Union. Many years before frontier settlers reached Minnesota, Native Americans inhabited the area. When settlers arrived, they pushed the Native Americans westward. In Minnesota's first state seal, a pioneer plowed the land while a Native American galloped away. During the 1960s, people began to question this depiction. It was criticized for representing the takeover of Native American land. Minnesotans wanted a seal that represented all citizens of the state, including Native Americans. The government made several changes to the seal throughout the years. The last change was made in 1983. Today the seal shows the Native American rider facing the farmer as he rides toward him. This shows that Minnesota celebrates all the different parts of its heritage.

1

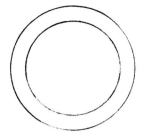

Draw two circles.

2

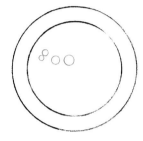

For the horse, draw two circles that touch each other. Draw another pair of circles that are bigger than the first pair.

3

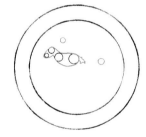

Connect the circles to outline the horse. Add the tail. For the men, draw a circle above the horse and another one next to the tail.

4

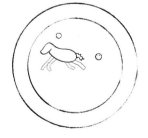

Erase extra lines and add four thin rectangles for the horse's legs.

5

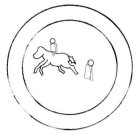

Add rectangles for the men's bodies. Now draw thinner rectangles for the men's arms.

6

Draw the men's legs. Now add a feather and ponytail to the Native American, and draw the farmer's hat. Add the horse's face and its ears.

7

Finish the men by adding a face on the Native American and hair on the farmer. Draw the horse's mane. Use a triangle and two rectangles to draw the farmer's plow.

8

Erase extra lines and smudges. Add as much detail and shading as you like. You can also add the words "THE GREAT SEAL OF THE STATE OF MINNESOTA", the year 1858, and the state motto.
Nice work!

The State Flag

Minnesota's state flag has the state seal centered against a blue background. Around the seal is the state flower, a wreath of lady slippers. There are 19 stars to show that Minnesota was the nineteenth state to join the Union after the original 13 colonies. The single, large, gold star represents Minnesota. There are three dates on the flag. On the top of the seal, 1858 is written, the year Minnesota became a state. On the left side is 1819, which stands for the year Fort Snelling was established, and 1893 is the year Minnesota had its first state flag. The flag that was adopted in 1893 was simplified, and the current flag was approved and officially adopted in 1957. The outside of the flag is trimmed in gold fringe.

1

Draw a large rectangle for the flag.

2

Outline the top, the right side, and the bottom of the rectangle. These are the sides where there will be gold fringe.

3

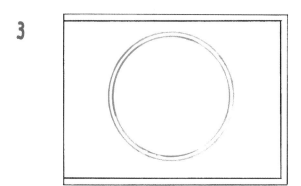

Add two large circles inside the flag. Try to center the circles in the middle.

4

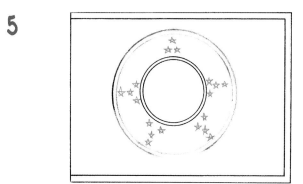

Add two smaller circles in the center of the first two circles.

5

Draw the stars between the inner and outer circles. Note the placement of the stars. Notice that there are three stars on the top and that the rest of the stars are grouped in fours.

6

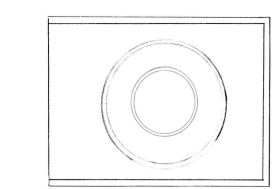

Write 1858 on the top center of the inner circle. Write "MINNESOTA" in the bottom center of the outer circle. To draw the rest of the flag, refer to the Minnesota state seal instructions from the previous chapter.

The Pink and White Lady Slipper

Minnesota's state flower is the pink and white lady slipper (*Cypripedium reginae*). It was adopted in 1902. Lady slippers are in the orchid family, and there are four varieties. These flowers are called lady slippers because that is what they look like! They have white petals and a larger, pink-and-white petal that looks like a pouch. The flower's leaves are hairy and can cause bad rashes if touched. Lady slippers grow from one to three flowers on a plant stalk that is from 1 to 2 feet (30–61 cm) tall. They grow slowly, and it takes 4 to 16 years for their first flower to blossom. Lady slippers are rare and it is illegal to pick them. They have been protected by Minnesota law since 1925.

1

Start with a circle for the center of the flower.

2

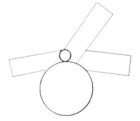

Next add a large circle right under the small circle.

3

For the petals, draw three rectangles as shown in the red highlights. Notice how the rectangles fan out from the two circles.

4

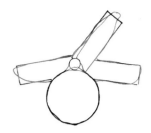

Soften the lines of the rectangles. Round off the sharp corners with curves.

5

Shape the large, round circle into a more oval shape. This is the pouchy-looking, large petal. Erase extra lines. Now draw a long thin rectangle for the flower's stem.

6

Add shading and detail to your flower, and you're done.

The Red Pine

The red pine (*Pinus resinosa*), also known as the red Norway pine, became the state tree in 1953. It is called the red pine because of its reddish brown bark. The bark has wide, flat scales. Red pine needles grow in pairs of two. They are green and are from 4 to 6 inches (10–15 cm) long. The cones of the red pine are about 2 inches (5 cm) long and are light brown in color. The tree stands from 60 to 100 feet (18–30 m) tall, and its trunk is from 3 to 5 feet (1–1.5 m) wide. The tallest red pine in Minnesota stands 120 feet (36.5 m) and is more than 300 years old. It has been alive 150 years longer than Minnesota has been a state!

1

Draw a long, thin triangle for the tree trunk.

2

Draw a shorter, but wider, triangle over the first triangle. Draw this triangle lightly because it is only a guide to help you fill out the tree. You will erase it later.

3

To add branches, draw lines from the tree trunk to the edge of the outer triangle. Notice how the branches are not straight and also how they fork and split in different directions.

4

You can add more branches than the drawing above to make your tree look fuller. Once you've finished the branches, erase the wider triangle.

5

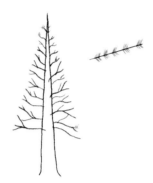

Draw short, straight lines on all the branches to create the tree's needles. Before you start, check out the close-up drawing of the needles on the branch. The more needles you draw, the fuller your tree will look.

6

The last step is to shade the tree. You just drew the red pine tree!

The Common Loon

Minnesota accepted the common loon as its state bird in 1961. The word "loon" comes from a Norwegian word which means "a wild, sad cry," which is the sound a loon makes. Loons are one of Earth's oldest living species and date from 60 million years ago! Minnesota is home to more than 12,000 loons. Loons are about 3 feet (1 m) long and have a wingspan of 5 feet (1.5 m). The loon has a black head, a black-and-white body, and a white underbelly. Loons are good swimmers and divers but are clumsy on land. Loons mate for life and lay from two to three eggs every year in the same area. After a month, the babies hatch. They take to the water within two days. Loons like to eat fish, especially trout.

1

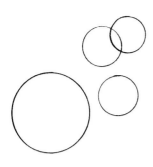

Draw four circles. Pay attention to the placement of the circles. Notice that one of the circles is almost three times bigger than the other three circles. Also notice that two of the smaller circles overlap.

2

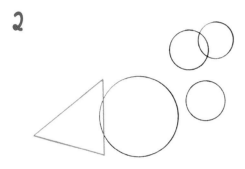

For the loon's tail, draw a triangle that slightly overlaps the big circle.

3

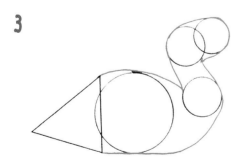

Use the circles and the triangle as a guide to draw the shape of the loon.

4

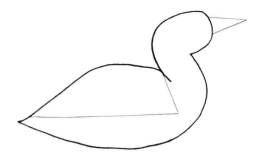

Erase the extra lines. Now draw a triangle for the beak. For the shape of the loon's wing, draw the angled shape as shown.

5

Soften the shape of the beak and wing. Erase extra lines. Draw a small circle for the eye. Right under the loon's body, draw a wavy line for the water.

6

Add shading and detail to the loon. To make the water look more real, shade the area underneath the loon, and then smudge it with your fingertips. Nice job!

Fort Snelling

In 1819, Colonel Josiah Snelling and the Fifth Regiment Infantry of the U.S. Army staked an area between the Mississippi River and the Minnesota River to build Fort Snelling. They had come to the unsettled area to make sure that only American citizens used the land. Even though the land had been purchased from France in 1803, it was only after the War of 1812 that the U.S. government claimed the area. Outposts, like Fort Snelling, were built all across the new American frontier to govern the territory. For more than 30 years, Fort Snelling was a meeting place for fur traders, Native Americans, soldiers, and travelers. In 1960, Fort Snelling became the first National Historic Landmark in the state.

1

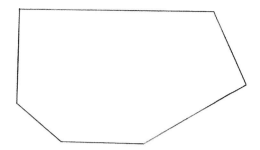

Start by drawing the fort's outline. Study the shape carefully before you start. Notice that there are six sides to the shape. Also notice that the six sides are not all the same length.

2

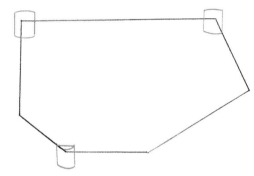

Add three rounded rectangles.

3

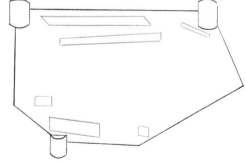

Erase extra lines. For the buildings inside the fort, draw six rectangles. Notice that the rectangles are all shaped differently. Also note their placement inside the fort.

4

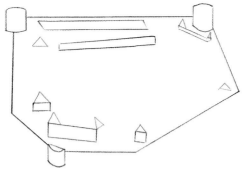

In this step, you will draw eight triangles for the building roofs. First draw six triangles on top of the rectangles. Then draw a triangle on the left corner and another triangle on the right corner of the fort's outline.

5

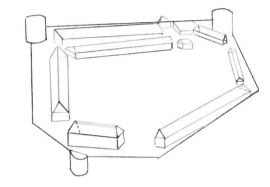

Look at the red highlighted lines above. Now make the same lines in your drawing to connect the triangles. Use the building drawing technique you just learned to add four more buildings as shown above in the fort's upper right corner.

6

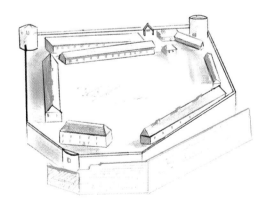

For the outer wall, use the technique you just learned. Start with three rectangles, and then connect them with lines. Add shading and detail to the fort, and you're done!

The Gopher

The gopher is Minnesota's official mascot. There are 35 gopher species, and they are found only in North America and in Central America. Gophers have powerful legs that they use to dig tunnels, so that they can live underground in burrows. They have toes with five digits. Each digit has a claw that helps them dig and move underground. Gophers can move both forward and backward, because their tails have special sensors that alert them of anything that may block their way. Gophers have big pockets in each cheek, which they use to transport food under ground to store. Gophers eat roots and plants. They sometimes cause problems when they dig up people's yards!

1

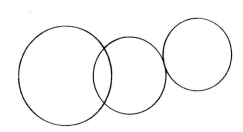

Draw three circles for the basic shape of the gopher's body. Notice how two of the circles overlap.

2

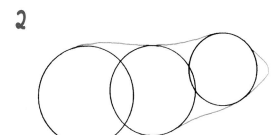

Connect the circles to form the body, and add a little bump for the gopher's nose.

3

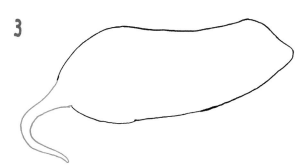

Erase the extra lines. Use curved lines to draw the tail.

4

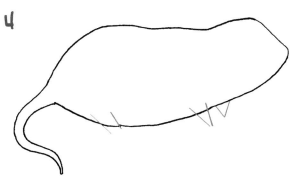

Use two triangles near the head to start the shape of the front legs, and add two short lines for the rear leg.

5

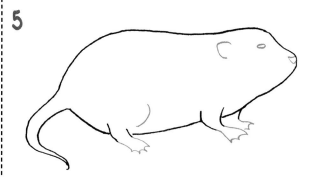

Use the triangles and the two lines to shape the gopher's feet. Draw its eye, ear, and nose.

6

Add shading and detail to your gopher, and you're done. You can also add whiskers and short lines in its body to give it a furry look.

25

The Giant Beaver

The giant beaver (*Casturoides ohioensis*) became Minnesota's official state fossil in 1988. Giant beavers were one of the largest rodents ever to live. They became extinct about 10,000 years ago. The giant beaver was about 6 feet (2 m) long, three times the size of today's beaver. It was nearly the size of a black bear! It is believed that giant beavers weighed about 480 pounds (218 kg). They had large, ridged cutting teeth that measured ½ inch (1 cm) on the top and 2 inches (5 cm) on the bottom. Giant beavers had deep skulls and rounded tails. Giant beavers lived in the Great Lakes area during the Ice Age, from about 12,500 to 11,800 years ago.

1

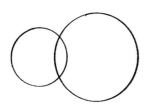

Draw two circles for the basic shape of the giant beaver's body.

2

Add a slanted rectangle for the giant beaver's head.

3

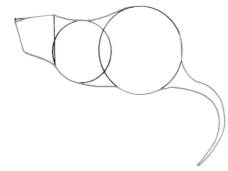

Connect the two circles and the rectangle to outline the giant beaver's body. Next draw its tail.

4

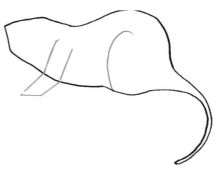

Erase extra lines. Add two rectangles for the front leg and a curved line for the rear leg.

5

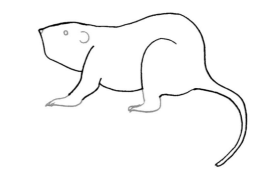

Draw the giant beaver's feet and add its eye, ear, and nose.

6

Add whiskers and short lines to its body to give it a furry look. After shading, your drawing is done!

Minnesota's Capitol

Minnesota's capitol, built in 1896, is located in St. Paul. Minnesota's first capitol burned down in 1881. The second capitol, built in 1883, was too small for the state's growing government. In 1893, the state held a nationwide competition for a new capitol design. The design of a young architect named Cass Gilbert was chosen. After he built the Minnesota capitol in the Renaissance style, Gilbert went on to build many other famous buildings, including the Supreme Court Building in Washington, D.C. Minnesota's capitol was built using granite from St. Cloud, Minnesota, and marble from Georgia. It measures 434 feet by 229 feet (132 m x 70 m).

1

Draw three rectangles. Notice that the middle rectangle is wider than the right and left rectangles.

2

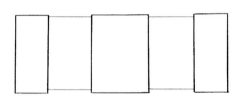

Connect the rectangles with four lines. After you are done with these lines, you should have five rectangles. Notice that the second and fourth rectangles are slightly shorter than the other rectangles.

3

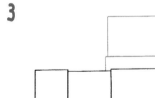

Draw two more rectangles to form the base of the dome.

4

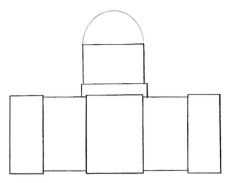

Draw a half circle for the dome.

5

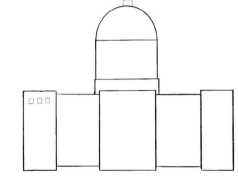

Draw a much smaller half circle on top of the first half circle. Now add a small triangle for the dome's peak. Start drawing the windows with small squares.

6

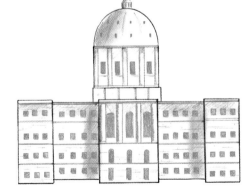

Add the pole on top of the dome. Continue to draw small square windows. Now add detail to the building, including the columns. Shade the drawing, and you are done!

Minnesota State Facts

Statehood	May 11, 1858, 32nd state
Area	86,943 square miles (225,181 sq km)
Population	4,725,000
Capital	St. Paul, population, 259,600
Most Populated City	Minneapolis, population, 362,700
Industries	Real estate, health services, insurance, industrial machinery, publishing, scientific equipment, food processing
Agriculture	Corn, soybeans, hogs, dairy products, cattle, turkey, wheat
Fossil	*Casturoides ohioensis* (giant beaver)
Bird	Common loon
Mushroom	Morel
Fish	Walleye
Motto	*L'Etoile du Nord*, Star of the North
Tree	Red pine
Gemstone	Lake Superior agate
Insect	Monarch butterfly
Song	"Hail! Minnesota"
Muffin	Blueberry muffin
Grain	Wild rice
Drink	Milk

Glossary

burrows (BUR-ohz) Holes in the ground made by animals and used for shelter.

commercial (kuh-MER-shul) Relating to business or trade.

contiguous (kun-TIH-gyoo-us) Having contact with.

depiction (dih-PIKT-shun) An image of something.

development (dih-VEH-lup-mint) Growth.

digits (DIH-jits) Fingers and toes.

extinct (ik-STINKT) No longer existing.

French and Indian War (FRENCH AND IN-dee-in WOR) A war fought between England and France over North American land from 1754 to 1763.

granite (GRA-niht) Melted rock that cooled and hardened beneath Earth's surface.

Ice Age (YS AYJ) A period of time about 12,000 years ago.

Louisiana Purchase (loo-EE-zee-a-nuh PER-ches) Land that the United States bought from France in 1803 that included the present state of Minnesota.

mascot (MAS-kaht) A person, an animal, or an object that is used by a group of people to represent them.

Renaissance style (REH-nuh-sahns STYL) A style of design that began in Italy in the 1400s and 1500s.

rodents (ROH-dents) Small animals, usually with sharp teeth for chewing.

scales (SKAYLZ) Small, flat, rounded sections covering a tree's trunk.

sensors (SEN-serz) A part of the body that can hear, see, smell, or feel things.

species (SPEE-sheez) A single kind of plant or animal.

stalk (STAHK) The slender part of the plant that supports other parts.

wreath (REETH) A circle of leaves and sometimes flowers woven together.

Index

Web Sites

For more information about Minnesota, check out this Web site:
www.state.mn.us